Sing a Song
of Popcorn

Sing a Song of Popcorn

EVERY CHILD'S BOOK OF POEMS

Illustrated by nine Caldecott Medal artists

MARCIA BROWN

LEO and DIANE DILLON

RICHARD EGIELSKI

TRINA SCHART HYMAN

ARNOLD LOBEL

MAURICE SENDAK

MARC SIMONT

MARGOT ZEMACH

Selected by Beatrice Schenk de Regniers
Eva Moore • Mary Michaels White • Jan Carr

SCHOLASTIC INC.   NEW YORK

In memory of
ARNOLD LOBEL

Library of Congress Cataloging-in-Publication Data
Sing a song of popcorn.
Rev. ed. of: Poems children will sit still for. 1969.
Includes indexes.
Summary: A collection of 128 poems by a variety of well-known
authors with illustrations by nine Caldecott medalists.
1. Children's poetry. [1. American poetry—Collections.
2. English poetry—Collection] I. de Regniers, Beatrice Schenk.
II. Moore, Eva.   III. White, Mary Michaels.   IV. Carr, Jan.
ill. Hyman, Trina Schart, et al.   Poems children will sit still for.
PN6109.97.S36   1988   808.81   87-4330

ISBN 0-590-40645-0

12 11 10 9 8 7 6 5 4 3 2 1   8 9/8 0 1 2 3/9

Printed in Italy
First Scholastic Printing, September 1988

Acknowledgments

Grateful acknowledgment is made to the following authors, agents, and publishers for the use of copyrighted materials. Every effort has been made to obtain permission to use previously published material. Any errors or omissions are unintentional.

Association for Childhood Education International and David Ross for "Good Morning" by Muriel Sipe (Mrs. David Ross) from SUNG UNDER THE SILVER UMBRELLA, copyright 1935 by The Macmillan Company.

Atheneum Publishers for "8 A.M. Shadows" from 8 A.M. SHADOWS by Patricia Hubbell, copyright © 1965 by Patricia Hubbell; "What in the World?" and "To Meet Mr. Lincoln" from THERE IS NO RHYME FOR SILVER by Eve Merriam, copyright © 1962 by Eve Merriam; "On Our Way," "Big Little Boy," "Weather," from CATCH A LITTLE RHYME by Eve Merriam, copyright © 1966 by Eve Merriam; "To a Red Kite" from I THOUGHT I HEARD THE CITY by Lilian Moore, copyright © 1969 by Lilian Moore; "Until I Saw the Sea" and "Night Creature" from SOMETHING NEW BEGINS, copyright © 1982 by Lilian Moore.

A.S. Barnes & Company, Inc., for "A Funny Man" by Natalie Joan from BARNES BOOK OF NURSERY VERSE.

Rowena Bennett for "The Steam Shovel" and five lines from "The Witch of Willowby Wood" from STORY-TELLER POEMS, copyright 1948 by Rowena Bennett.

Bobbs-Merrill Co., for "K,"."C," "R," "X," and "Z," from CERTAINLY, CARRIE, CUT THE CAKE by Margaret and John Travers Moore, copyright © 1971 by Margaret and John Travers Moore.

William Cole for "Here Comes the Band" by William Cole and for "Oh Did You Hear?" by Shel Silverstein, © 1961 by Shel Silverstein.

Collins-Knowlton-Wing, Inc., for "The Pumpkin" from A GOLDEN LAND by Robert Graves, copyright © 1959 by Robert Graves.

Curtis Brown for "Lengths of Time" from WONDERFUL TIME by Phyllis McGinley, text copyright © 1965, 1966 by Phyllis McGinley.

Doubleday & Company, Inc., for "The Bat" from THE COLLECTED POEMS OF THEODORE ROETHKE, copyright 1938 by Theodore Roethke; and "Mice" by Rose Fyleman from FIFTY-ONE NEW NURSERY RHYMES, copyright 1932 by Doubleday & Company, Inc.

E.P. Dutton & Company, Inc., for "Day Before Christmas," copyright 1941 by Marchette Chute from RHYMES ABOUT THE COUNTRY by Marchette Chute; "Dogs," copyright 1946 by Marchette Chute, and "Weather," copyright 1941 by Marchette Chute, from AROUND AND ABOUT by Marchette Chute, published 1957 by E.P. Dutton & Company, Inc; "Galoshes" from STORIES TO BEGIN ON by Rhoda W. Bacmeister, copyright 1940 by E.P. Dutton & Company, Inc., renewal © 1968 by Rhoda W. Bacmeister; "Politeness" from WHEN WE WERE VERY YOUNG by A.A. Milne, copyright 1924 by E.P. Dutton & Company, Inc. Renewal 1952 by A.A. Milne; "Furry Bear" from NOW WE ARE SIX by A.A. Milne, copyright 1927 by E.P. Dutton & Company, Inc. Renewal © 1955 by A.A. Milne; "The More It Snows" from THE HOUSE AT POOH CORNER by A.A. Milne, copyright 1928 by E.P. Dutton & Company, Inc. Renewal © 1956 by A.A. Milne; "A Pig Tale," "W," and "The Old Wife and the Ghost" from THE BLACKBIRD IN THE LILAC by James Reeves, published 1959 by E.P. Dutton & Company, Inc.

Norma Millay Ellis for "Come along in then, little girl" from "From a Very Little Sphinx" from COLLECTED POEMS OF EDNA ST. VINCENT MILLAY, copyright 1929, 1956 by Edna St. Vincent Millay and Norma Millay Ellis, published by Harper & Row, Publishers.

Follett Publishing Company for "Necks," "Tails," "Gingerbread Man," and "When You Talk to a Monkey" from THE DAY IS DANCING by Rowena Bennett, copyright © 1948, 1968 by Rowena Bennett.

Samuel French, Inc., for "Snail" by John Drinkwater.

Harcourt, Brace & World, Inc., for "Arithmetic" (excerpt), "We Must Be Polite," "Paper I," and "Paper II" from COMPLETE POEMS by Carl Sandburg, copyright 1950 by Carl Sandburg; "Buffalo Dusk" from SMOKE AND STEEL by Carl Sandburg, copyright 1920 by Harcourt, Brace & World, Inc., renewed 1948 by Carl Sandburg; "who knows if the moon's...," copyright 1925 by e.e. cummings from POEMS 1923–1954 by e.e. cummings; "If We Walked On Our Hands" from SOMETHING SPECIAL by Beatrice Schenk de Regniers, © 1958 by Beatrice Schenk de Regniers.

Harper & Row, Publishers for "I Have a Lion" and "If I Were a..." (last stanza) from THE ROSE ON MY CAKE by Karla Kuskin, copyright © 1964 by Karla Kuskin; "Knitted Things" from ALEXANDER SOAMES: HIS POEMS by Karla Kuskin, copyright © 1962 by Karla Kuskin.

Contents

SPOOKY POEMS · Margot Zemach (39)

STORY POEMS · Maurice Sendak (49)

MOSTLY PEOPLE · Marc Simont (83)

MOSTLY NONSENSE · Richard Egielski (103)

SEEING, FEELING, THINKING · Leo and Diane Dillon (113)

IN A FEW WORDS · *Marcia Brown* (127)

Introduction

I have been asked to tell something about the history of this book—how it all began, almost twenty years ago.

History? We weren't making history—Eva Moore, Mary White, and I. We were making a collection—a collection of poems that children would enjoy listening to over and over; that teachers would have a good time reading aloud to the class.

The three of us, along with Grace Loud, our secretary, were the staff of Lucky Book Club, Scholastic's paperback book program for second- and third-graders. For all of us, Lucky Book Club was more than a job. It was our passion. Our mission: to bring the joy of reading to our Lucky children. We worked with publishers to get reprint rights to books we wanted for our Lucky readers. We worked with writers—novice and established writers—to create new books.

Eva Moore and I had always believed that children and poetry belonged together. Many teachers, we knew, would be happy to make poetry an integral part of the school day. But along with everything else teachers had to do, where and how could they look for poems that would be surefire hits with their children?

Well, we three Lucky editors would do the job for them! We would put together an irresistible collection of poems. What was more, this collection would be unlike any other. So many anthologies, we had noted, seemed to be anthologies of anthologies, so that the same poems were anthologized over and over. We would go to original sources—to collections of poems by individual poets. For example, rather than take Carl Sandburg's often anthologized "Fog," we would go to collections of his poetry and find something that would be fresh for the teacher as well as for the children. On the other hand, Eva Moore reminded us, we must not be so rigid that we would omit poems that were too good to miss, such as Laura E. Richard's "Eletelephony."

The three of us read aloud to each other the poems any one of us wanted considered. We listened with our grown-up selves and with our seven- and eight-year-old selves. Our threshold of boredom was low. We were ruthless: "Well, I can see why you like that poem," one of us would say, "but I don't think a roomful of kids will sit still for it." Finally, we had 106 poems and a title: *Poems Children Will Sit Still For: a Selection for the Primary Grades.*

Just as a poem must have a shape, a collection of poems must have a shape, too. So we took the 106 poems and fooled around with them, putting them into categories: Fun with Rhymes, Mostly Animals, Mostly People, Mostly Nonsense, and so forth.

The categories, or sections, were not watertight. Poetry is fluid and spills over from one category into another. "Brother," for example, by Mary Ann Hoberman, could have been included in Fun with Rhymes as easily as in the section Mostly People. No committee looked over our shoulders. No one told us we must be sure to have certain poets or certain kinds of poems, or to avoid certain kinds of poems. We were given— or we took—the kind of autonomy under which we worked best. The book really did seem to fill a need. It sold over a quarter of a million copies.

In 1983, fourteen years after the book was first published (and about two years after I left Scholastic to concentrate on my own writing), it was decided to add a number of poems as well as some new poets to the collection; to drop a few poems; juggle some of the categories—in short, to update the collection but still maintain its original intent. An illustrator would also be chosen.

There were a number of projects in the works at Scholastic, and nothing was done on this one for several years. Then Eva Moore (now editor of Lucky Book Club) worked with Associate Editor Jan Carr to select additional poems and to get the book ready for illustration. By now it was clear that the book should not be limited to the classroom. After all, if a classroom of thirty children would sit still for the poems, so would any one child.

So the book shed its school uniform: Off with the old title. On with a new title that would make clear that this was a joyous collection that belonged in every home with a child in it. The format was enlarged to give scope to the illustrations. Jean Feiwel, Scholastic's editor-in-chief, decided to have different artists illustrate each section. In fact, if such a coup was possible, each section would be illustrated by a Caldecott Medal artist.

Now, almost two decades after it was first conceived, the little book has achieved a kind of apotheosis, with illustrations by nine celebrated Caldecott Medal artists, each illustration expanding the meaning and pleasure of the poems. This is the first time the work of these nine artists has appeared together between the covers of a single book.

Still, there is something missing. To my mind, a poem is not completed until it is read aloud. Some people can read a music score and hear the music. Many people can read a poem silently and hear its music. But it seems to me that the full power of a poem—the jazzy rhythms, the lyrical cadence, the dance of language, the sheer pleasure of fooling around with sound and meaning—can be fully appreciated only if the poem is read aloud. This would be particularly true for children.

So do take time to read these poems aloud. Use your normal tone of voice. The advice the Duchess gave Alice (in Wonderland) is as good as any: "Take care of the sense, and the sounds will take care of themselves." (The advice works just as well the other way 'round for some nonsense poems.) Just remember that if you enjoy the poem, your listener is likely to enjoy it, too.

For this book particularly, what Jorge Luis Borges says of reading in general applies: "It should be for happiness."

Happy reading!

—Beatrice Schenk de Regniers

Sing a Song
of Popcorn

Trina Schart Hyman

FUN
WITH
RHYMES

from
JAMBOREE

A rhyme for ham? *Jam.*
A rhyme for mustard? *Custard.*
A rhyme for steak? *Cake.*
A rhyme for rice? *Another slice.*
A rhyme for stew? *You.*
A rhyme for mush? *Hush!*
A rhyme for prunes? *Goons.*
A rhyme for pie? *I.*
A rhyme for iced tea? *Me.*
For the pantry shelf? *Myself.*

David McCord

W

The King sent for his wise men all
    To find a rhyme for W;
When they had thought a good long time
But could not think of a single rhyme,
"I'm sorry," said he, "to trouble you."

James Reeves

A
Kettle's for the kitchen,
A key is for the door,
A kitten is for playing with
And keeping on the floor.

A kite is made for flying
When March winds blow,
Kindness is for everyone —
Didn't you know?

Certainly, Carrie, cut the cake —
Cut it carefully, goodness' sake:
Cherries for the children,
Chestnuts (a few)
And chocolate, chocolate just for you!

R is for ribbon,
a rose
and a ring,
a ruby,
a raindrop
and a robin in spring!

What words begin with X?
Very few.
X-ray and xylophone
Will do.

In winter when it's
Zero
I zoom straight home from play,
But when the springtime sun is bright
I zig-zag
all
the
way!

Margaret and John Travers Moore

WHAT THEY SAID

It's four o'clock,
Said the cock.

It's still dark,
Said the lark.

What's that?
Said the cat.

I want to sleep,
Said the sheep.

A bad habit,
Said the rabbit.

Of course,
Said the horse.

Let's have a spree,
Said the bee.

But where?
Said the hare.

In the barrow,
Said the sparrow.

I'm too big,
Said the pig.

In the house,
Said the mouse.

But the dog said — Bow-wow,
It's too late now.

German nursery rhyme translated
by Rose Fyleman

MY NAME IS…

My name is Sluggery-wuggery
My name is Worms-for-tea
My name is Swallow-the-table-leg
My name is Drink-the-sea.
My name is I-eat-saucepans
My name is I-like-snails
My name is Grand-piano-George
My name is I-ride-whales.
My name is Jump-the-chimney
My name is Bite-my-knee
My name is Jiggery-pokery
And Riddle-me-ree,
and ME.

Pauline Clarke

I WANT YOU TO MEET…

…Meet Ladybug,
her little sister Sadiebug,
her mother, Mrs. Gradybug,
her aunt, that nice oldmaidybug,
and Baby — she's a fraidybug.

David McCord

A PIG TALE

Poor Jane Higgins.
She had five piggins,
And one got drowned in the Irish Sea.
Poor Jane Higgins,
She had four piggins,
And one flew over the sycamore tree.
Poor Jane Higgins,
She had three piggins,
And one was taken away for pork.
Poor Jane Higgins,
She had two piggins,
And one was sent to the Bishop of Cork.
Poor Jane Higgins,
She had one piggin,
And that was struck by a shower of hail,
So poor Jane Higgins,
She had no piggins,
And that's the end of my little pig tale.

James Reeves

FIVE LITTLE SQUIRRELS

Five little squirrels
Sat in a tree.
The first one said,
"What do I see?"
The second one said,
"A man with a gun."
The third one said,
"We'd better run."
The fourth one said,
"Let's hide in the shade."
The fifth one said,
"*I'm* not afraid."
Then BANG went the gun,
And how they did run!

Unknown

LULU, LULU, I'VE A LILO

*Charlotte Pomerantz
has fun with rhymes
in different languages.
This poem introduces
four words from
the Samoan language.*

Owl, owl,
I've a secret.
And I am to blame.
I lost my brand-new handkerchief.
Isn't that a shame?
But you can't tell my secret, owl.
You don't know my name.

Lulu, lulu,
I've a lilo.
And I am to blame.
I lost my brand-new solosolo.
Isn't that a shame?
But you can't tell my lilo, lulu.
You don't know my name.

Charlotte Pomerantz

WHERE DO THESE
WORDS COME FROM?

*All of the English
words in this rhyming
chant are derived
from Native American
languages.*

Hominy, succotash, raccoon, moose.
Succotash, raccoon, moose, papoose.
Raccoon, moose, papoose, squash, skunk.
Moose, papoose, squash, skunk, chipmunk.
Papoose, squash, skunk, chipmunk, muckamuck.
Skunk, chipmunk, muckamuck, woodchuck.

Charlotte Pomerantz

Marcia Brown

MOSTLY
WEATHER

SO LONG AS THERE'S WEATHER

Whether it's cold
or
whether it's hot,
I'd rather
have weather
whether or not
   it's just what I'd choose.

Summer
or
Spring
or
Winter
or
Fall —
any weather
is better
than
no weather
at all.
   I really like weather.

I never feel
whiney
when weather is
rainy.
And when it's
sunshiny
I don't feel
complainy.
   Weather sends me.

(continued on page 15)

WEATHER

Dot a dot dot   dot a dot dot
Spotting the windowpane.
Spack a spack speck   flick a flack fleck
Freckling the windowpane.

A spatter a scatter   a wet cat a clatter
A splatter a rumble outside.
Umbrella umbrella umbrella umbrella
Bumbershoot barrel of rain.

Slosh a galosh   slosh a galosh
Slither and slather a glide
A puddle a jump a puddle a jump
A puddle a jump puddle splosh
A juddle a pump aluddle a dump a
Puddmuddle jump in and slide!

Eve Merriam

So —
Rain?
Let it SPLASH!
Thunder?
CRRRASH!
Hail?
Clitter-clatter!
What does it
matter —
    so long as there's weather!

Tamara Kitt

WEATHER

It is a windy day.
The water's white with spray.
And pretty soon, if this keeps up,
The world will blow away.

Marchette Chute

CLOUDS

White sheep, white sheep
On a blue hill,
When the wind stops
You all stand still.
When the wind blows
You walk away slow.
White sheep, white sheep,
Where do you go?

Christina G. Rossetti

RAIN

The rain is raining all around,
It falls on field and tree,
It rains on the umbrellas here,
And on the ships at sea.

Robert Louis Stevenson

RAIN, RAIN, GO AWAY

Rain, rain, go away.
Come again some other day.
Little Johnny wants to play.

Unknown

GALOSHES

Susie's galoshes
Make splishes and sploshes
And slooshes and sloshes
As Susie steps slowly
Along in the slush.

They stamp and they tramp
On the ice and concrete,
They get stuck in the muck and the mud;
But Susie likes much best to hear

The slippery slush
As it slooshes and sloshes,
And splishes and sploshes,
All around her galoshes!

Rhoda Bacmeister

I HEARD A BIRD SING

I heard a bird sing
   In the dark of December
A magical thing
   And sweet to remember.
"We are nearer to Spring
   Than we were in September,"
I heard a bird sing
   In the dark of December.

Oliver Herford

APRIL RAIN SONG

Let the rain kiss you.
Let the rain beat upon your head with
   silver liquid drops.
Let the rain sing you a lullaby.
The rain makes still pools on the sidewalk.
The rain makes running pools in the gutter.
The rain plays a little sleep-song on our roof at night.
And I love the rain.

Langston Hughes

(20)

LO, THE WINTER IS PAST

For, lo, the winter is past.
The rain is over and gone.
The flowers appear on the earth.
The time of the singing birds is come.

The Bible

THE MORE IT SNOWS

The more it
SNOWS-tiddely-pom,
The more it
GOES-tiddely-pom
The more it
GOES-tiddely-pom
On
Snowing.

And nobody
KNOWS-tiddely-pom,
How cold my
TOES-tiddely-pom
How cold my
TOES-tiddely-pom
Are
Growing.

A. A. Milne

FURRY BEAR

If I were a bear,
   And a big bear too,
I shouldn't much care
   If it froze or snew;
I shouldn't much mind
   If it snowed or friz —
I'd be all fur-lined
   With a coat like his!

For I'd have fur boots and a brown fur wrap,
And brown fur knickers and a big fur cap.
I'd have a fur muffle-ruff to cover my jaws,
And brown fur mittens on my big brown paws.
With a big brown furry-down up to my head,
I'd sleep all the winter in a big fur bed.

A. A. Milne

from
A POPCORN SONG

Sing a song of popcorn
    When the snowstorms rage;
Fifty little round men
    Put into a cage.
Shake them till they laugh and leap
    Crowding to the top;
Watch them burst their little coats
    Pop!! Pop!! Pop!!

                    Nancy Byrd Turner

SNOWFLAKES

Sometime this winter if you go
To walk in soft new-falling snow
When flakes are big and come down slow

To settle on your sleeve as bright
As stars that couldn't wait for night,
You won't know what you have in sight —

Another world — unless you bring
A magnifying glass. This thing
We call a snowflake is the king

Of crystals. Do you like surprise?
Examine him three times his size:
At first you won't believe your eyes.

Stars look alike, but flakes do not:
No two the same in all the lot
That you will get in any spot

You chance to be, for every one
Come spinning through the sky has none
But his own window-wings of sun:

Joints, points, and crosses. What could make
Such lacework with no crack or break?
In billion billions, no mistake?

David McCord

FIRST SNOW

Snow makes whiteness where it falls.
The bushes look like popcorn-balls.
The places where I always play
Look like somewhere else today.

Marie Louise Allen

SUNFLAKES

If sunlight fell like snowflakes,
gleaming yellow and so bright,
we could build a sunman,
we could have a sunball fight,
we could watch the sunflakes
drifting in the sky.
We could go sleighing
in the middle of July
through sundrifts and sunbanks,
we could ride a sunmobile,
and we could touch sunflakes —
I wonder how they'd feel.

Frank Asch

FOUR SEASONS

Spring is showery, flowery, bowery.
Summer: hoppy, croppy, poppy.
Autumn: wheezy, sneezy, freezy.
Winter: slippy, drippy, nippy.

Unknown

OUR TREE

When spring comes round, our apple tree
    Is very full of flowers,
And when a bird sits on a branch
    The petals fall in showers.

When summer comes, our apple tree
    Is very full of green,
And everywhere you look in it
    There is a leafy screen.

When autumn comes, our apple tree
    Is full of things to eat.
The apples hang from every branch
    To tumble at our feet.

When winter comes, our apple tree
    Is full of snow and ice
And rabbits come to visit it…
    We think our tree is nice.

Marchette Chute

THE NORTH WIND DOTH BLOW

The north wind doth blow
And we shall have snow,
And what will poor robin do then, poor thing?
  He'll sit in a barn,
   And keep himself warm,
And hide his head under his wing, poor thing!

The north wind doth blow
And we shall have snow,
And what will the dormouse do then, poor thing?
  Roll'd up like a ball,
   In his nest snug and small,
He'll sleep till warm weather comes in, poor thing!

The north wind doth blow
And we shall have snow,
And what will the children do then, poor things?
  When lessons are done,
   They must skip, jump, and run,
Until they have made themselves warm, poor things!

Unknown

DRAGON SMOKE

Breathe and blow
white clouds
     with every puff.
It's cold today,
     cold enough
to see your breath.
Huff!
     Breathe dragon smoke
     today!

Lilian Moore

RAIN POEM

The rain was like a little mouse,
quiet, small and gray.
It pattered all around the house
and then it went away.

It did not come, I understand,
indoors at all, until
it found an open window and
left tracks across the sill.

Elizabeth Coatsworth

RAIN

Summer rain
is soft and cool,
so I go barefoot
in a pool.

But winter rain
is cold, and pours,
so I must watch it
from indoors.

Myra Cohn Livingston

WIND SONG

When the wind blows
the quiet things speak.
Some whisper, some clang,
Some creak.

Grasses swish.
Treetops sigh.
Flags slap
and snap at the sky.
Wires on poles
whistle and hum.
Ashcans roll.
Windows drum.

When the wind goes —
suddenly
then,
the quiet things
are quiet again.

Lilian Moore

WHO HAS SEEN THE WIND?

Who has seen the wind?
  Neither I nor you.
But when the leaves hang trembling,
  The wind is passing through.

Who has seen the wind?
  Neither you nor I.
But when the trees bow down their heads,
  The wind is passing by.

Christina G. Rossetti

TO A RED KITE

Fling
yourself
upon the sky.

Take the string
you need.
Ride high,

high
above the park.
Tug and buck
and lark
with the wind.

Touch a cloud,
red kite.
Follow the wild geese
in their flight.

Lilian Moore

WINDY NIGHTS

Whenever the moon and stars are set,
   Whenever the wind is high,
All night long in the dark and wet,
   A man goes riding by.
Late in the night when the fires are out,
Why does he gallop and gallop about?

Whenever the trees are crying aloud,
   And ships are tossed at sea,
By, on the highway, low and loud,
   By at the gallop goes he.
By at the gallop he goes, and then
By he comes back at the gallop again.

Robert Louis Stevenson

(35)

STOPPING BY WOODS ON A SNOWY EVENING

Whose woods these are I think I know.
His house is in the village though;
He will not see me stopping here
To watch his woods fill up with snow.

My little horse must think it queer
To stop without a farmhouse near
Between the woods and frozen lake
The darkest evening of the year.

He gives his harness bells a shake
To ask if there is some mistake.
The only other sound's the sweep
Of easy wind and downy flake.

The woods are lovely, dark and deep.
But I have promises to keep,
And miles to go before I sleep,
And miles to go before I sleep.

Robert Frost

Margot Zemach

SPOOKY
POEMS

THE OLD WIFE AND THE GHOST

There was an old wife and she lived all alone
   In a cottage not far from Hitchin:
And one bright night, by the full moon light,
   Comes a ghost right into her kitchen.

About that kitchen neat and clean
   The ghost goes pottering round.
But the poor old wife is deaf as a boot
   And so hears never a sound.

The ghost blows up the kitchen fire,
   As bold as bold can be;
He helps himself from the larder shelf,
   But never a sound hears she.

He blows on his hands to make them warm,
   And whistles aloud "Whee-hee!"
But still as a sack the old soul lies
   And never a sound hears she.

From corner to corner he runs about,
   And into the cupboard he peeps;
He rattles the door and bumps on the floor,
   But still the old wife sleeps.

Jangle and bang go the pots and pans,
   As he throws them all around;
And the plates and mugs and dishes and jugs,
   He flings them all to the ground.

Madly the ghost tears up and down
   And screams like a storm at sea;
And at last the old wife stirs in her bed —
   And it's "Drat those mice," says she.

(continued on page 42)

Then the first cock crows and morning shows
    And the troublesome ghost's away.
But oh! what a pickle the poor wife sees
    When she gets up next day.

"Them's tidy big mice," the old wife thinks,
    And off she goes to Hitchin,
And a tidy big cat she fetches back.
    To keep the mice from her kitchen.

James Reeves

from
THE WITCH OF WILLOWBY WOOD

There once was a witch of Willowby Wood,
and a weird wild witch was she, with hair that was snarled
and hands that were gnarled, and a kickety, rickety
knee. She could jump, they say,
to the moon and back, but this I never did see.

Rowena Bennett

THE PUMPKIN

You may not believe it, for hardly could I:
I was cutting a pumpkin to put in a pie,
And on it was written in letters most plain
"You may hack me in slices, but I'll grow again."

I seized it and sliced it and made no mistake
As, with dough rounded over, I put it to bake:
But soon in the garden as I chanced to walk,
Why, there was that pumpkin entire on his stalk!

Robert Graves

THE BAT

By day the bat is cousin to the mouse.
He likes the attic of an aging house.

His fingers make a hat about his head.
His pulse beat is so slow we think him dead.

He loops in crazy figures half the night
Among the trees that face the corner light.

But when he brushes up against a screen,
We are afraid of what our eyes have seen:

For something is amiss or out of place
When mice with wings can wear a human face.

Theodore Roethke

from
KNITTED THINGS

There was a witch who knitted things:
Elephants and playground swings.
She knitted rain,
She knitted night,
But nothing really came out right.
The elephants had just one tusk
And night looked more
Like dawn or dusk.

Karla Kuskin

SOMEONE

Someone came knocking
  At my wee, small door,
Someone came knocking,
  I'm sure—sure—sure;
I listened, I opened,
  I looked to left and right,
But nought there was a-stirring
  In the still dark night.
Only the busy beetle
  Tap-tapping in the wall,

Only from the forest
  The screech-owl's call,
Only the cricket whistling
  While the dew drops fall,
So I know not who came knocking,
  At all, at all, at all.

Walter de la Mare

STORY POEMS

THE GINGERBREAD MAN

The gingerbread man gave a gingery shout:
"Quick! Open the oven and let me out!"
He stood up straight in his baking pan.
He jumped to the floor and away he ran.
"Catch me," he called, "if you can, can, can."

The gingerbread man met a cock and a pig
And a dog that was brown and twice as big
As himself. But he called to them all as he ran,
"You can't catch a runaway gingerbread man."

The gingerbread man met a reaper and sower.
The gingerbread man met a thresher and mower;
But no matter how fast they scampered and ran
They couldn't catch up with a gingerbread man.

Then he came to a fox and he turned to face him.
He dared Old Reynard to follow and chase him;
But when he stepped under the fox's nose
Something happened. What do you s'pose?
The fox gave a snap. The fox gave a yawn,
And the gingerbread man was gone, gone, GONE.

Rowena Bennett

THE JUMBLIES

I

They went to sea in a sieve, they did,
   In a sieve they went to sea:
In spite of all their friends could say,
On a winter's morn, on a stormy day,
   In a sieve they went to sea!
And when the sieve turned round and round,
And everyone cried, "You'll all be drowned!"
They called aloud, "Our sieve ain't big,
But we don't care a button! We don't care a fig!
   In a sieve we'll go to sea!"
      Far and few, far and few,
         Are the lands where the Jumblies live;
         Their heads are green, and their hands are blue,
            And they went to sea in a sieve.

II

They sailed away in a sieve, they did,
  In a sieve they sailed so fast,
With only a beautiful pea-green veil
Tied with a riband by way of a sail,
  To a small tobacco-pipe mast.
And everyone said, who saw them go,
"O won't they be soon upset, you know!
For the sky is dark, and the voyage is long,
And happen what may, it's extremely wrong
  In a sieve to sail so fast!"
    Far and few, far and few,
      Are the lands where the Jumblies live;
      Their heads are green, and their hands are blue,
        And they went to sea in a sieve.

III

The water it soon came in, it did,
  The water it soon came in;
So to keep them dry, they wrapped their feet
In a pinky paper all folded neat,
  And they fastened it down with a pin.
And they passed the night in a crockery-jar,
And each of them said, "How wise we are!
Though the sky be dark, and the voyage be long,
Yet we never can think we were rash or wrong,
  While round in our sieve we spin!"
      Far and few, far and few,
        Are the lands where the Jumblies live;
        Their heads are green, and their hands are blue,
        And they went to sea in a sieve.

IV

And all night long they sailed away;
   And when the sun went down,
They whistled and warbled a moony song,
To the echoing sound of a coppery gong,
   In the shade of the mountains brown.
"O Timballo! How happy we are,
When we live in a sieve and a crockery-jar!
And all night long in the moonlight pale,
We sail away with a pea-green sail,
   In the shade of the mountains brown!"
      Far and few, far and few,
        Are the lands where the Jumblies live;
        Their heads are green, and their hands are blue,
        And they went to sea in a sieve.

V

They sailed to the Western Sea, they did,
   To a land all covered with trees,
And they bought an owl, and a useful cart,
And a pound of rice, and a cranberry tart,
   And a hive of silvery bees.
And they bought a pig, and some green jackdaws,
And a lovely monkey with lollipop paws,
And forty bottles of Ringo-Bo-Ree,
   And no end of Stilton cheese.
      Far and few, far and few,
        Are the lands where the Jumblies live;
        Their heads are green, and their hands are blue,
        And they went to sea in a sieve.

VI

And in twenty years they all came back,
   In twenty years or more,
And everyone said, "How tall they've grown!
For they've been to the Lakes, and the Torrible Zone,
   And the hills of the Chankly Bore;"
And they drank their health, and gave them a feast
Of dumplings made of beautiful yeast;
And everyone said, "If we only live,
We too will go to sea in a sieve —
   To the hills of the Chankly Bore!"
     Far and few, far and few,
      Are the lands where the Jumblies live;
     Their heads are green, and their hands are blue,
      And they went to sea in a sieve.

Edward Lear

THERE WAS A CROOKED MAN

There was a crooked man
And he walked a crooked mile;
He found a crooked sixpence
Beside a crooked stile;
He bought a crooked cat
And it caught a crooked mouse
And they both lived together
In a wee crooked house.

Nursery Rhyme

from
ADVENTURES OF ISABEL

Isabel met an enormous bear,
Isabel, Isabel, didn't care;
The bear was hungry, the bear was ravenous,
The bear's big mouth was cruel and cavernous.
The bear said, Isabel, glad to meet you,
How do, Isabel, now I'll eat you!
Isabel, Isabel, didn't worry,
Isabel didn't scream or scurry.
She washed her hands and she straightened her
  hair up,
Then Isabel quietly ate the bear up.

Once in a night as black as pitch
Isabel met a wicked old witch.
The witch's face was cross and wrinkled,
The witch's gums with teeth were sprinkled.
Ho ho, Isabel! the old witch crowed,
I'll turn you into an ugly toad!
Isabel, Isabel, didn't worry,
Isabel didn't scream or scurry.
She showed no rage and she showed no rancor,
But she turned the witch into milk and drank her.

Isabel met a hideous giant,
Isabel continued self-reliant.
The giant was hairy, the giant was horrid,
He had one eye in the middle of his forehead.
Good morning, Isabel, the giant said,
I'll grind your bones to make my bread.
Isabel, Isabel, didn't worry,
Isabel didn't scream or scurry.
She nibbled the zwieback that she always fed off,
And when it was gone, she cut the giant's head off.

Ogden Nash

Arnold Lobel

MOSTLY
ANIMALS

GOOD MORNING

One day I saw a downy duck,
With feathers on his back;
I said, "Good morning, downy duck,"
And he said, "Quack, quack, quack."

One day I saw a timid mouse,
He was so shy and meek;
I said, "Good morning, timid mouse,"
And he said, "Squeak, squeak, squeak."

One day I saw a curly dog,
I met him with a bow;
I said, "Good morning, curly dog,"
And he said, "Bow-wow-wow."

One day I saw a scarlet bird,
He woke me from my sleep;
I said, "Good morning, scarlet bird,"
And he said, "Cheep, cheep, cheep."

Muriel Sipe

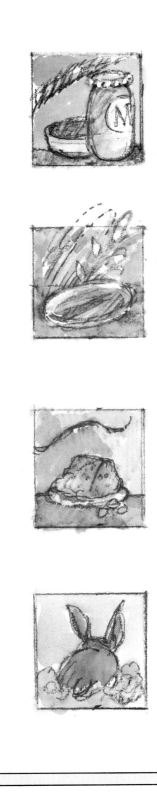

WHAT IN THE WORLD?

What in the world
goes whiskery friskery
meowling and prowling
napping and lapping
at silky milk?

Psst,
What is it?

What in the world
goes leaping and beeping
onto a lily pad onto a log
onto a tree stump or down to the bog?

Splash, blurp,
Kerchurp!

What in the world
goes gnawing and pawing
scratching and latching
sniffing and squiffing
nibbling for tidbits of left-over cheese?
Please?

What in the world
jumps with a hop and a bump
and a tail that can thump
has pink pointy ears and a twitchy nose
looking for anything crunchy that grows?
A carroty lettucey cabbagey luncheon
To munch on?

What in the world
climbs chattering pattering swinging from trees
like a flying trapeze
with a tail that can curl
like the rope the cowboys twirl?
Wahoo!
Here's a banana for you!

What in the world
goes stalking and balking
running and sunning
thumping and dumping
lugging and hugging
swinging and singing
wriggling and giggling
sliding and hiding
throwing and knowing and
growing and growing
much too big for
last year's clothes?
Who knows?

Eve Merriam

THE MYSTERIOUS CAT

I saw a proud, mysterious cat,
I saw a proud, mysterious cat,
Too proud to catch a mouse or rat —
Mew, mew, mew.

But catnip she would eat, and purr,
But catnip she would eat, and purr.
And goldfish she did much prefer —
Mew, mew, mew.

I saw a cat — 'twas but a dream,
I saw a cat — 'twas but a dream,
Who scorned the slave that brought her cream —
Mew, mew, mew.

Unless the slave were dressed in style,
Unless the slave were dressed in style,
And knelt before her all the while —
Mew, mew, mew.

Did you ever hear of a thing like that?
Did you ever hear of a thing like that?
Did you ever hear of a thing like that?
Oh, what a proud mysterious cat.
Oh, what a proud mysterious cat.
Oh, what a proud mysterious cat.
Mew…Mew…Mew.

Vachel Lindsay

MY CAT, MRS. LICK-A-CHIN

Some of the cats I know about
Spend a little time in and a lot of time out.
Or a lot of time out and a little time in.
But *my* cat, Mrs. Lick-a-chin,
Never knows *where* she wants to be.
If I let her in she looks at me
And begins to sing that she wants to go out.
So I open the door and she looks about
And begins to sing, "Please let me in!"

Poor silly Mrs. Lick-a-chin!

The thing about cats, as you may find,
Is that no one knows what they have in mind.

And I'll tell you something about that;
No one knows it less than my cat.

John Ciardi

FROM A VERY LITTLE SPHINX

Come along in then, little girl!
  Or else stay out!
But in the open door she stands,
And bites her lip and twists her hands,
And stares upon me, trouble-eyed;
"Mother," she says, "I can't decide!"

Edna St. Vincent Millay

I HAVE A LION

I had a cat,
Gray
Soft
Fat
Given to grrrring
Quite softly
And prrrrring.
Slipped off one morning
Near the green glen.
That was my cat
Who was not seen again.

I had a dog,
Noisy and yellow
Very cold nose
Wonderful fellow.
Trotted one evening
Out after a pack
Of dog-footed friends
And never came back.

I had a bird,
Bright blue in a cage
Sang without cause
On his miniature stage.
Sat on my shoulder
Looked in my eye.
Sailed out the window
And into the sky.

I have a lion,
Furry and kind
Sits on a shelf
Near the autos that wind.
Eyes wild and golden
Tail like a tuft
He never will slip out and leave me.
He's stuffed.

Karla Kuskin

DOGS

The dogs I know
Have many shapes.
For some are big and tall,
  And some are long,
  And
  some
  are thin,
And some are fat and small.

And some are little bits of fluff
And have no shape at all.

Marchette Chute

THE CAMEL

The camel has a single hump;
The dromedary, two;
Or else the other way around.
I'm never sure. Are you?

Ogden Nash

NECKS

The swan has a neck that is curly and long.
The camel has one that is shaggy and strong.
But the spotted giraffe
Has a neck and a half.

Rowena Bennett

WHEN YOU TALK TO A MONKEY

When you talk to a monkey
   He seems very wise.
He scratches his head,
   And he blinks both his eyes;
But he won't say a word.
   He just swings on a rail
And makes a big question mark
   Out of his tail.

Rowena Bennett

TAILS

The kangaroo has a heavy tail
   She sits on for a chair.
There's scarcely any tail at all
   Upon the polar bear.
But the monkey has the nicest tail
   Of any living thing,
For he can hook it to a branch
   And use it as a swing.

Rowena Bennett

WHO LIVED IN A SHOE?

You know that old woman
  Who lived in a shoe?
She had so many children
  She didn't know what to do?

I think if she lived in
  A little shoe-house
That little old lady was
  Surely a mouse!

Beatrix Potter

MICE

I think mice
Are rather nice.
  Their tails are long,
  Their faces small,
  They haven't any
  Chins at all.
  Their ears are pink,
  Their teeth are white,
  They run about
  The house at night.
  They nibble things
  They shouldn't touch
  And no one seems
  To like them much.
But I think mice
Are nice.

Rose Fyleman

TO A SQUIRREL AT KYLE-NA-NO

Come play with me.
Why should you run
Through the shaking tree
As though I'd a gun
To strike you dead?
When all I would do
Is to scratch your head
And let you go.

William Butler Yeats

LITTLE SNAIL

I saw a little snail
Come down the garden walk.
He wagged his head this way…that way…
Like a clown in a circus.
He looked from side to side
As though he were from a different country.
I have always said he carries his house on his back…
Today in the rain
I saw that it was his umbrella!

Hilda Conkling

SNAIL

Snail upon the wall,
Have you got at all
Anything to tell
About your shell?

Only this, my child —
When the wind is wild,
Or when the sun is hot,
It's all I've got.

John Drinkwater

THE DUCK

Behold the duck.
It does not cluck.
A cluck it lacks.
It quacks.
It is specially fond
Of a puddle or pond.
When it dines or sups,
It bottoms ups.

Ogden Nash

THE LITTLE TURTLE

There was a little turtle.
He lived in a box.
He swam in a puddle.
He climbed on the rocks.

He snapped at a mosquito.
He snapped at a flea.
He snapped at a minnow.
And he snapped at me.

He caught the mosquito.
He caught the flea.
He caught the minnow.
But he didn't catch me.

Vachel Lindsay

THE PRAYER OF THE LITTLE DUCKS

Dear God,
give us a flood of water.
Let it rain tomorrow and always.
Give us plenty of little slugs
and other luscious things to eat.
Protect all who quack
and every one who knows how to swim.

Amen

Carmen Bernos de Gasztold
translated from the French by *Rumer Godden*

GRANDPA BEAR'S LULLABY

The night is long
But fur is deep.
You will be warm
In winter sleep.

The food is gone
But dreams are sweet
And they will be
Your winter meat.

The cave is dark
But dreams are bright
And they will serve
As winter light.
Sleep, my little cubs, sleep.

Jane Yolen

FIREFLY

A little light is going by,
Is going up to see the sky,
A little light with wings.

I never could have thought of it,
To have a little bug all lit
And made to go on wings.

Elizabeth Maddox Roberts

THE CATERPILLAR

Brown and furry
Caterpillar in a hurry;
Take your walk
To the shady leaf or stalk.

May no toad spy you,
May the little birds pass by you;
Spin and die,
To live again a butterfly.

Christina G. Rossetti

HURT NO LIVING THING

Hurt no living thing;
Ladybird, nor butterfly,
Nor moth with dusty wing,
Nor cricket chirping cheerily,
Nor grasshopper so light of leap,
Nor dancing gnat, nor beetle fat,
Nor harmless worms that creep.

Christina G. Rossetti

PACHYCEPHALOSAURUS (*pak-i-sef-a-lo-saw-rus*)

Among the later dinosaurs
   Though not the largest, strongest,
PACHYCEPHALOSAURUS had
   The name that was the longest.

Yet he had more than syllables,
   As you may well suppose.
He had great knobs upon his cheeks
   And spikes upon his nose.

Ten inches thick, atop his head,
   A bump of bone projected.
By this his brain, though hardly worth
   Protecting, was protected.

No claw or tooth, no tree that fell
   Upon his head kerwhacky,
Could crack or crease or jar or scar
   That stony part of Paky.

And so he nibbled plants in peace
   And lived untroubled days.
Sometimes, in fact, as Paky proved,
   To be a bonehead pays.

Richard Armour

THE STEAM SHOVEL

The steam digger
Is much bigger
Than the biggest beast I know.
He snorts and roars
Like the dinosaurs
That lived long years ago.

He crouches low
On his tractor paws
And scoops the dirt up
With his jaws;
Then swings his long
Stiff neck around
And spits it out
Upon the ground…

Oh, the steam digger
Is much bigger
Than the biggest beast I know.
He snorts and roars
Like the dinosaurs
That lived long years ago.

Rowena Bennett

BUFFALO DUSK

The buffaloes are gone.
And those who saw the buffaloes are gone.
Those who saw the buffaloes by thousands and
    how they pawed the prairie sod into dust
    with their hoofs, their great heads down
    pawing on in a great pageant of dusk,
Those who saw the buffaloes are gone.
And the buffaloes are gone.

Carl Sandburg

FOR A BIRD

I found him lying near the tree;
    I folded up his wings.
    Oh, little bird,
    You never heard
    The song the summer sings.

I wrapped him in a shirt I wore in winter;
    it was blue.
    Oh, little bird,
    You never heard
    The song I sang to you.

Myra Cohn Livingston

M Simont

MOSTLY
PEOPLE

ON OUR WAY

What kind of walk shall we take today?
Leap like a frog? Creep like a snail?
Scamper like a squirrel with a furry tail?

Flutter like a butterfly? Chicken peck?
Stretch like a turtle with a poking-out neck?

Trot like a pony, clip clop clop?
Swing like a monkey in a treetop?

Scuttle like a crab? Kangaroo jump?
Plod like a camel with an up-and-down hump?

We could even try a brand-new way —
Walking down the street
On our own two feet.

Eve Merriam

BIG LITTLE BOY

"Me oh my," said the tiny, shiny ant,
"I can crawl all the way up a sand hill,
A hill so high it's as big as a thimble.
Can any creature in the world be bigger than I?"

"Skat," said the green caterpillar,
"I can inch myself all the way across a twig.
Now a twig is really *big*!
Hooray for great, glorious, mammoth, and modest me."

"Gog and magog," said the speckled frog,
"And bilge water. Little ant, crawly caterpillar,
You can only creep.
I can leap!
All the way up to a tremendous lily pad in the pond.
How superiffic can any creature be?
I'll tell you —
He can be me!"

"Oh," laughed the little boy,
"Gangway, skedaddle, vamoose.
Look at me, tiny ant. My finger is bigger than a
    thimble.
Look, inchy caterpillar. My foot is bigger than a twig.
Look, speckled frog. My hand can cover a lily pad all
    over.
Why, I'm so big I can run in circles, I can run in
    squares,

I can reach to tables, I can fill up chairs!
And I'm still growing!
When I grow all the way up, my head will bump the
    sky.
I'll have clouds for a bed, and a moon pillow,
And stars instead of freckles on my nose."

(*Is that how big a little boy grows?*)

Eve Merriam

LENGTHS OF TIME

Time is peculiar
And hardly exact.
Though minutes are minutes,
You'll find for a fact
(As the older you get
And the bigger you grow)
That time can
Hurrylikethis
Or plod, plod, slow.

Waiting for your dinner when you're hungry?
Down with the sniffles in your bed?
Notice how an hour crawls along and crawls along
Like a snail with his house upon his head.

But when you are starting
A game in the park,
It's morning,
It's noon,
And suddenly it's dark.
And hours like seconds
Rush blurringly by,
Whoosh!
Like a plane in the sky.

Phyllis McGinley

DAY BEFORE CHRISTMAS

We have been helping with the cake
    And licking out the pan,
And wrapping up our packages
    As neatly as we can.
And we have hung our stockings up
    Beside the open grate.
And now there's nothing more to do
    Except
        to
            wait!

Marchette Chute

HERE COMES THE BAND

The band comes booming down the street,
The tuba oomphs, the flutes tweet tweet;
The trombones slide, the trumpets blare,
The baton twirls up in the air.
There's "ooh's!" and "ahs!" and cheers and
    clapping —
And I can't stop my feet from tapping.

William Cole

KNOXVILLE, TENNESSEE

I always like summer
best
you can eat fresh corn
from daddy's garden
and okra
and greens
and cabbage
and lots of
barbecue
and buttermilk
and homemade ice-cream
at the church picnic

and listen to
gospel music
outside
at the church
homecoming
and go to the mountains with
your grandmother
and go barefooted
and be warm
all the time
not only when you go to bed
and sleep

Nikki Giovanni

TO MEET MR. LINCOLN

If I lived at the time
That Mr. Lincoln did,
And I met Mr. Lincoln
With his stovepipe lid

And his coalblack cape
And his thundercloud beard,
And worn and sad-eyed
He appeared:

"Don't worry, Mr. Lincoln,"
I'd reach up and pat his hand,
"We've got a fine President
For this land;

And the Union will be saved,
And the slaves will go free;
And you will live forever
In our nation's memory."

Eve Merriam

from
ARITHMETIC

Arithmetic is where numbers fly
  like pigeons in and out of your head.
Arithmetic tells you how many you lose or win
  if you know how many you had
  before you lost or won.
Arithmetic is seven eleven all good children
  go to heaven — or five six bundle of sticks.
Arithmetic is numbers you squeeze from your
  head to your hand to your pencil to your paper
  till you get the right answer....
If you have two animal crackers, one good and one bad,
  and you eat one and a striped zebra
  with streaks all over him eats the other,
  how many animal crackers will you have
  if somebody offers you five six seven and you say
  No no no and you say Nay nay nay
  and you say Nix nix nix?
If you ask your mother for one fried egg
  for breakfast and she gives you
  two fried eggs and you eat
  both of them, who is better in arithmetic,
  you or your mother?

Carl Sandburg

PAPER I

Paper is two kinds, to write on, to wrap with.
If you like to write, you write.
If you like to wrap, you wrap.
Some papers like writers, some like wrappers.
Are you a writer or a wrapper?

Carl Sandburg

PAPER II

I write what I know on one side of the paper
    and what I don't know on the other.
Fire likes dry paper and wet paper laughs at
    fire.
Empty paper sacks say, "Put something in me,
    what are we waiting for?"
Paper sacks packed to the limit say, "We hope
    we don't bust."
Paper people like to meet other paper people.

Carl Sandburg

BEGINNING ON PAPER

on paper
I write it
on rain

I write it
on stones
on my boots

on trees
I write it
on the air

on the city
how pretty
I write my name

Ruth Krauss

(95)

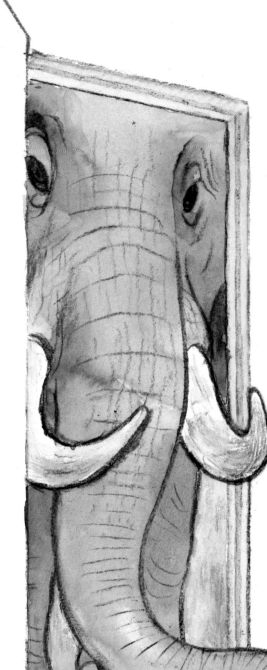

WE MUST BE POLITE

(*Lessons for children on how to
behave under peculiar circumstances*)

If we meet a gorilla
what shall we do?
Two things we may do
if we so wish to do.

Speak to the gorilla,
very, very respectfully,
"How do you do, sir?"

Or, speak to him with less
distinction of manner,
"Hey, why don't you go back
where you came from?"

If an elephant knocks on your door
and asks for something to eat,
there are two things to say:

Tell him there are nothing but cold
victuals in the house and he will do
better next door.

Or say: We have nothing but six bushels
of potatoes — will that be enough for
your breakfast, sir?

Carl Sandburg

POLITENESS

If people ask me,
I always tell them:
"Quite well, thank you, I'm very glad to say."
If people ask me,
I always answer,
"Quite well, thank you, how are you today?"
I always answer,
I always tell them,
If they ask me,
Politely....
BUT SOMETIMES
   I wish
      That they wouldn't.

A. A. Milne

THERE'S SOMEONE I KNOW

There's someone I know
whom I simply can't stand,
I wish he would bury
his head in the sand,

or move to the moon
or to deep outer space,
whenever I see him
I make a weird face.

Today during recess
outside in the yard,
he suddenly gave me
a valentine card.

I wish that he hadn't,
it made me upset,
it's the prettiest one
I could possibly get.

Jack Prelutsky

MY FAVORITE WORD

There is one word —
My favorite —
The very, very best.
It isn't No or Maybe.
It's Yes, Yes, Yes, *Yes,* YES!

"Yes, yes, you may," and
"Yes, of course," and
"Yes, please help yourself."
And when I want a piece of cake,
"Why, yes. It's on the shelf."

Some candy? "Yes."
A cookie? "Yes."
A movie? "Yes, we'll go."

I love it when they say my word:
Yes, *Yes, YES! (Not No.)*

Lucia and James L. Hymes, Jr.

TREE HOUSE

A tree house, a free house,
A secret you and me house,
A high up in the leafy branches
Cozy as can be house.

A street house, a neat house,
Be sure and wipe your feet house
Is not my kind of house at all —
Let's go live in a tree house.

Shel Silverstein

BROTHER

I had a little brother
And I brought him to my mother
And I said I want another
Little brother for a change.
But she said don't be a bother
So I took him to my father
And I said this little bother
Of a brother's very strange.

But he said one little brother
Is exactly like another
And every little brother
Misbehaves a bit he said.
So I took the little bother
From my mother and my father
And I put the little bother
Of a brother back to bed.

Mary Ann Hoberman

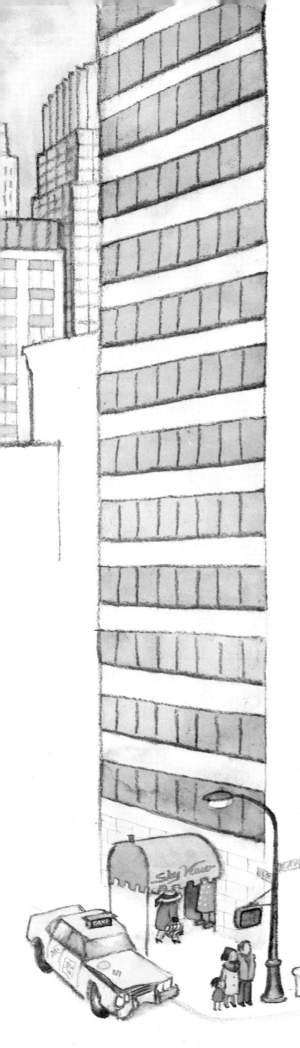

HOUSES

The homes of our
Earliest ancestors
Were lower than low.
They had no windows.
They had no doors.
If you wished to go in
You went on all fours —
The dirt or the dust
Or the snow was the floor.
It was hundreds and hundreds
Of years before
Men lived in houses
With windows and doors
Or lay down in beds
Or sat up in chairs
Or sat down at table
Or walked upstairs:
Then, as time goes,
It was no time at all
Before houses were built
So exceedingly tall,
They had hundreds of windows
And only one door
And you had to go up
In an elevator.
And now they have grown
So gigantically high
They nudge the new moon
And scrape the blue sky;
And today we live
Like bees in a hive
In the tallest cities
That Mister Man
Has built on this earth
Since the world began.

Mary Britton Miller

Richard Egielski

MOSTLY
NONSENSE

OH DID YOU HEAR?

Oh did you hear?
The President has measles,
The Principal has just burned down the school,
Your hair is filled with jam
    and purple weasels

April Fool!

Shel Silverstein

IF I WERE A...

If I were a sandwich,
I'd sit on a plate
And think of my middle
Until someone ate
Me.
End of the sandwich.

Karla Kuskin

NICHOLAS NED

Nicholas Ned,
    He lost his head,
And put a turnip on instead;
    But then, ah, me!
    He could not see,
So he thought it was night, and he went to bed.

Laura E. Richards

IF WE WALKED ON OUR HANDS

If we walked on our hands
   instead of our feet
And we all ate paper
   instead of meat
What a mixed-up place this world would be.
What a mixed-up
   fixed-up
   topsy-turvy
   sit-u-a-tion.

If we wore our hats
   on our behinds
And all we ate
   were melon rinds
What a mixed-up place this world would be.
What a mixed-up
   fixed-up
   topsy-turvy
   sit-u-a-tion.

If babies worked
   while papas played
If the children gave orders
   and parents obeyed
What a mixed-up place this world would be.
What a mixed-up
   fixed-up
   topsy-turvey
   sit-u-a-tion.

Beatrice Schenk de Regniers

A FUNNY MAN

One day a funny kind of man
Came walking down the street.
He wore a shoe upon his head,
And hats upon his feet.

He raised the shoe and smiled at me,
His manners were polite;
But never had I seen before
Such a funny-sounding sight.

He said, "Allow me to present
Your Highness with a rose."
And taking out a currant bun
He held it to my nose.

I staggered back against the wall,
And then I answered, "Well!
I never saw a rose with such
A funny-looking smell."

He then began to sing a song,
And sat down on the ground;
You never heard in all your life
Such a funny-feeling sound.

"My friend, why do you wear two hats
Upon your feet?" I said.
He turned the other way about,
And hopped home on his head.

Natalie Joan

THE FOLK WHO LIVE IN
BACKWARD TOWN

The folk who live in Backward town
Are inside out and upside down.
They wear their hats inside their heads
And go to sleep beneath their beds.
They only eat the apple peeling
And take their walks across the ceiling.

Mary Ann Hoberman

ELETELEPHONY

Once there was an elephant,
Who tried to use the telephant —
No! No! I mean an elephone
Who tried to use the telephone —
(Dear me! I am not certain quite
That even now I've got it right.)

Howe'er it was, he got his trunk
Entangled in the telephunk;
The more he tried to get it free,
The louder buzzed the telephee —
(I fear I'd better drop the song
Of elephop and telephong!)

Laura E. Richards

THE SPAGHETTI NUT

Eddie the spaghetti nut
courted pretty Nettie Cutt.
They wed and Ed and Nettie got
a cottage in Connecticut.

Eddie said to Nettie, "Hot
spaghetti I've just got to get."
So Nettie put it in a pot
and cooked spaghetti hot and wet.

Nettie cut spaghetti up
for Eddie in Connecticut.
Eddie slurped it from a cup,
that hot spaghetti Nettie cut.

Then Eddie, Nettie and their cat
that Nettie called Spaghettipet
all sat in the spaghetti vat —
so much for their spaghettiquette.

Jack Prelutsky

(109)

OLD MAN AND THE COW

There was an Old Man who said, "How
Shall I flee from this horrible Cow?
   I will sit on this stile,
   And continue to smile,
Which may soften the heart of that Cow."

Edward Lear

OLD MAN OF PERU

There was an old man of Peru
Who dreamed he was eating his shoe.
   He woke in the night
   In a terrible fright,
And found it was perfectly true.

Unknown

A YOUNG FARMER OF LEEDS

There was a young farmer of Leeds
Who swallowed six packets of seeds.
   It soon came to pass
   He was covered with grass,
And he couldn't sit down for the weeds.

Unknown

A YOUNG LADY FROM GLITCH

There was a young lady from Glitch
Who tried to turn into a witch.
   But she found that the most
   She could be was a ghost,
So she threw herself into a ditch.

Tamara Kitt

Leo Dillon   Diane Dillon

SEEING,
FEELING,
THINKING

WHAT IS PINK?

What is pink? a rose is pink
By a fountain's brink.
What is red? a poppy's red
In its barley bed.
What is blue? the sky is blue
Where the clouds float thro'.
What is white? a swan is white
Sailing in the light.
What is yellow? pears are yellow,
Rich and ripe and mellow.
What is green? the grass is green,
With small flowers between.
What is violet? clouds are violet
In the summer twilight.
What is orange? why, an orange,
Just an orange!

Christina G. Rossetti

UNTIL I SAW THE SEA

Until I saw the sea
I did not know
that wind
could wrinkle water so.

I never knew
that sun
could splinter a whole sea of blue.

Nor
did I know before,
a sea breathes in and out
upon a shore.

Lilian Moore

POEM

I loved my friend.
He went away from me.
There's nothing more to say.
The poem ends,
Soft as it began —
I loved my friend.

Langston Hughes

8 A.M. SHADOWS

Everyone's shadow is taller than really,
The shadows of giants are taller than trees,
The shadows of children are big as their parents,
And shadows of trotting dogs bend at the knees.
Everyone's shadow is taller than really,
Everyone's shadow is thinner than thin,
8 a.m. shadows are long as the dawning,
Pulling the night away,
Coaxing the light to say:
"Welcome, all shadows,
Day, please begin!"

Patricia Hubbell

THE SWING

How do you like to go up in a swing,
Up in the air so blue?
Oh, I do think it is the pleasantest thing
Ever a child can do!

Up in the air and over the wall,
Till I can see so wide,
Rivers and trees and cattle and all
Over the countryside —

Till I look down on the garden green,
Down on the roof so brown —
Up in the air I go flying again,
Up in the air and down!

Robert Louis Stevenson

HOW TO TELL THE TOP OF A HILL

The top of a hill
Is not until
The bottom is below.
And you have to stop
When you reach the top
For there's no more UP to go.

To make it plain
Let me explain:
The one *most* reason why
You have to stop
When you reach the top — is:
The next step up is sky.

John Ciardi

who knows if the moon's

who knows if the moon's
a balloon, coming out of a keen city
in the sky — filled with pretty people?
(and if you and i should

get into it, if they
should take me and take you into their balloon,
why then
we'd go up higher with all the pretty people

than houses and steeples and clouds:
go sailing
away and away sailing into a keen
city which nobody's ever visited, where

always
   it's
       Spring) and everyone's
in love and flowers pick themselves

e.e. cummings

NIGHT CREATURE

I like
the quiet breathing
of the night,

the tree talk
the wind-swish
the star light.

Day is
glare-y
loud
scary.
Day bustles.

Night rustles.
I like
night.

Lilian Moore

MRS. PECK-PIGEON

Mrs. Peck-Pigeon
Is picking for bread,
Bob-bob-bob
Goes her little round head.
Tame as a pussy-cat
In the street,
Step-step-step
Go her little red feet.
With her little red feet
And her little round head,
Mrs. Peck-Pigeon
Goes picking for bread.

Eleanor Farjeon

A BIRD

A bird came down the walk,
He did not know I saw;
He bit an angleworm in halves
And ate the fellow, raw.

And then he drank a dew
From a convenient grass,
And then hopped sidewise to the wall
To let a beetle pass.

Emily Dickinson

FOXES

A litter of little black foxes. And later
A litter of little gray foxes. And later
A litter of little white foxes.
The white ones are lighter than gray.
Not a lot.
The gray ones are lighter than black.
Just a little.
The litters are lighter in moonlight.
They glitter.
They gleam in the moonlight. They glow and they glisten.
Out on the snow see the silver fox sparkle.

Mary Ann Hoberman

WINTER MOON

How thin and sharp is the moon tonight!
How thin and sharp and ghostly white
Is the slim curved crook of the moon tonight!

Langston Hughes

Marccia Brown

IN A FEW
WORDS

from
FIREFLY

I think
if you flew
up to the sky
beside the moon,
you would
twinkle
like a star.

Li Po

FIREFLIES

Fireflies at twilight
In search of one another
Twinkle off and on.

Mary Ann Hoberman

A MOTHER

A mother horse
Keeps watch
While her child
Drinks.

Issa

CONVERSATION

An umbrella
And a raincoat
Are walking and talking together.

Buson

(131)

SNOW MELTING

snow melting
broken shore
little pine tree

Ruth Krauss

MIRRORMENT

Birds are flowers flying
and flowers perched birds.

A. R. Ammons

ROCKS

Big rocks into pebbles,
pebbles into sand.
I really hold a million million rocks here in my hand.

Florence Parry Heide

SNOW

I could eat it!
This snow that falls
So softly, so softly.

Issa

Index of Titles

Index of First Lines

Index of Authors

(139)

About the Artists

Marcia Brown

Slogging home from school the longest way in the runniest gutters was a late winter delight of MARCIA BROWN'S childhood, "seeing just how deep you could go and not get a shock of ice water in your boots. For much of my childhood we lived where we could see thunderstorms coming across the valley with great gray veils of rain hiding one landmark after another."

Ms. Brown has been awarded the Caldecott Medal three times: in 1955 for *Cinderella,* in 1962 for *Once a Mouse,* and in 1983 for *Shadow.* She is well-known for her brilliant interpretations of folktales, and her illustrations for *Stone Soup, Puss in Boots,* and *The Steadfast Tin Soldiers* have all won Caldecott Honors. Born in Rochester, New York, she has traveled widely in Europe, the near and far east, and the United States, and now makes her home in West Redding, Connecticut.

Leo Dillon   Diane Dillon

LEO and DIANE DILLON came to children's books after many years of illustrating adult book jackets, album covers, and advertising material. They met at Parsons School of Design and competed with one another until they joined forces. Although they claim that working together did not come easy—"two egos and one piece of paper are a dangerous combination"—they have, nevertheless illustrated many outstanding picture books, including two Caldecott winners: *Why Mosquitos Buzz in People's Ears* and *Ashanti to Zulu: African Traditions.*

The poetry in the Dillon's section evoked so much feeling that they decided to do something completely different. Influenced by their new book of William Morris' fabric designs, they went for the essence of seeing, thinking, and feeling rather than being literal. "We wanted to leave the images a bit misty to give readers a chance to develop their own pictures."

Richard Egielski

RICHARD EGIELSKI grew up in New York City and attended the Pratt Institute and Parsons School of Design, where he studied with Maurice Sendak. It was Maurice Sendak who first inspired him to pursue a career in children's book illustration, and through him that he accidentally met his collaborator, the author Arthur Yorinks. Together, Mr. Egielski and Mr. Yorinks have produced several popular picture books, including *Hey Al*—the winner of the 1987 Caldecott Medal. Mr. Egielski illustrated Mostly Nonsense in a "straightforward, matter-of-fact manner, trying to ground fantasy in a kind of reality that would say to the reader, yes it sounds like nonsense, but see, it could happen."

Trina Schart Hyman

TRINA SCHART HYMAN grew up in and around Philadelphia where she illustrated her first book, self-written, at age four. She received her art training at the Philadelphia Museum College of Art in Stockholm, and the Boston Museum School. While on a recent visit with her daughter, Katrin, who is in the Peace Corps in Cameroon, Africa, Ms. Hyman found two children, Fatimatou and Dum-Dum, whom she used as models in this collection. The illustrator of more than seventy books, she won the Caldecott Medal in 1985 for *Saint George and the Dragon,* and a Caldecott Honor in 1984 for *Little Red Riding Hood*.

Arnold Lobel

Since he illustrated his first book, *Red Tag Comes Back,* in 1961, ARNOLD LOBEL has written and/or illustrated more than seventy books for children. A graduate of the Pratt Institute, he is as well-known for his stories as he is for his illustrations. His numerous award-winning books include *Hildilid's Night* and *Frog and Toad are Friends,* both Caldecott Honor Books; *Frog and Toad Together,* a Newbery Honor Book; and *Fables,* winner of the Caldecott Medal in 1981. After a long illness, he died on December 4, 1987, shortly after completing his artwork for *Sing a Song of Popcorn*.

Maurice Sendak

MAURICE SENDAK began his illustrious career doing window displays for the famous toy store, F.A.O. Schwarz. A writer, director, lyricist, and set and costume designer, he is perhaps the most celebrated children's book illustrator of his time. While illustrating this collection, Mr. Sendak vividly remembered moments of his childhood, one being that of "an early reader with odd but delectable yellow pictures of the gingerbread man. If recollection is to be trusted, I learned how to read from that lovely and musty smelling book. I can only wonder if my own gingerbread man bears the slightest resemblance to that bright yellow creature of long ago."

The author-illustrator of the 1964 Caldecott Medal winner *Where the Wild Things Are,* and Caldecott Honor books *In the Night Kitchen* and *Outside Over There,* he was awarded the Hans Christian Andersen Medal for his entire body of work, and the Laura Ingalls Wilder Award for his distinguished contribution to children's literature.

M Simont

MARC SIMONT was born in Paris of Spanish parents and spent his childhood in France, Spain, and the United States. Wherever he was, he was drawing. Mr. Simont usually found it easier to illustrate works where the narrative was dominant. So a poem with the magic of "Beginning on Paper" by Ruth Krauss provided him with a special challenge. He made several tries. "It was as if whenever I came close to touching it, it would disappear. I finally had to settle." A portrait painter, a caricature artist, an author, and a translator, he is best-known for his children's book illustrations. He received the Caldecott Medal in 1957 for *A Tree is Nice* and a Caldecott Honor in 1950 for *The Happy Day.*

Margot Zemach

MARGOT ZEMACH grew up in Los Angeles, California, attended the Los Angeles County Art Institute, and received a Fulbright scholarship to study at the Vienna Academy of Fine Arts. There, she met her late husband, Harvey Fischtrom, (an author under the name Harve Zemach). Together, the Zemachs produced several award-winning picture books, including *Duffy and the Devil: A Cornish Tale,* the winner of the Caldecott Medal in 1974. In 1978, Ms. Zemach won a Caldecott Honor for *It Could Always be Worse,* a book she wrote and illustrated. She has twice been nominated for the Hans Christian Andersen Medal—in 1980 and again in 1988. Used to working on books where you draw the same characters over and over, she found that illustrating poetry was a refreshing change. It was challenging to have to draw a bat with a man's face,—and her favorite piece of all—the spooky landscape that is the frontispiece of her section.

Jimenez